Basil Bunting

LOQUITUR

Fulcrum Press 16 Lawn Road London NW3

© Basil Bunting 1965

CONTENTS

OVERDRAFTS

PREFACE

The edition of my poems which Dallam Flynn printed in Texas in 1950 is all sold, and Stuart Montgomery thinks there are still people curious to read them who cannot find a copy. I have taken my chance to add two or three and take one away; to read the proofs more carefully than I could when I was in Teheran and my publisher in Texas; to insert a couplet in the Odes and promote The Orotava Road from limbo to its chronological place amongst them, which has obliged me to renumber many; and to give the book a title to replace the off-hand label by which it has been known or unknown for fifteen years.

All the poems have been in print and copyright for a long time, except the couplet, Ode 27. Many were first printed in *Poetry*, of Chicago, whose editors so many poets have had cause to thank. I want to record my gratitude to Dallam Flynn for the edition he undertook in a more difficult time than this, and my continual debt to the two greatest poets of our age, Ezra Pound and Louis Zukofsky. (I thank Jonathan Cape Ltd for letting me reprint 'In that this happening', so that people can look at Mr Zukofsky's poem and tell what my Latin is meant for.)

Basil Bunting

May 1965

SONATAS

VILLON

I

He whom we anatomized
"whose words we gathered as pleasant flowers
and thought on his wit and how neatly he described things"
speaks
to us, hatching marrow,
broody all night over the bones of a deadman.

My tongue is a curve in the ear. Vision is lies.
We saw it so and it was not so,
the Emperor with the Golden Hands, the Virgin in blue.
(—A blazing parchment,
Matthew Paris his kings in blue and gold.)

It was not so,
scratched on black by God knows who,
by God, by God knows who.

In the dark in fetters
on bended elbows I supported my weak back
hulloing to muffled walls blank again
unresonant. It was gone, is silent, is always silent.
My soundbox lacks sonority. All but inaudible
I stammer to my ear:
Naked speech! Naked beggar both blind and cold!
Wrap it for my sake in Paisley shawls and bright soft fabric,
wrap it in curves and cover it with sleek lank hair.

What trumpets? What bright hands? Fetters, it was the Emperor
with magic in darkness, I unforewarned.
The golden hands are not in Averrhoes,
eyes lie and this swine's fare bread and water
makes my head wuzz. Have pity, have pity on me!

To the right was darkness and to the left hardness
below hardness darkness above
at the feet darkness at the head partial hardness
with equal intervals without
to the left moaning and beyond a scurry.
In those days rode the good Lorraine
whom English burned at Rouen,
the day's bones whitening in centuries' dust.

Then he saw his ghosts glitter with golden hands,
the Emperor sliding up and up from his tomb
alongside Charles. These things are not obliterate.
White gobs spitten for mockery;
and I too shall have CY GIST written over me.

Remember, imbeciles and wits,
sots and ascetics, fair and foul,
young girls with little tender tits,
that DEATH is written over all.

Worn hides that scarcely clothe the soul
they are so rotten, old and thin,
or firm and soft and warm and full—
fellmonger Death gets every skin.

All that is piteous, all that's fair,
all that is fat and scant of breath,
Elisha's baldness, Helen's hair,
is Death's collateral:

Three score and ten years after sight
of this pay me your pulse and breath
value received. And who dare cite,
as we forgive our debtors, Death?

Abelard and Eloise,
Henry the Fowler, Charlemagne,
Genée, Lopokova, all these
die, die in pain.

And General Grant and General Lee,
Patti and Florence Nightingale,
like Tyro and Antiope
drift among ghosts in Hell,

know nothing, are nothing, save a fume
driving across a mind
preoccupied with this: Our doom
is, to be sifted by the wind,

heaped up, smoothed down like silly sands.
We are less permanent than thought.
The Emperor with the Golden Hands

is still a word, a tint, a tone,
insubstantial-glorious,
when we ourselves are dead and gone
and the green grass growing over us.

II

Let his days be few and let
his bishoprick pass to another,
for he fed me on carrion and on a dry crust,
mouldy bread that his dogs had vomited,
I lying on my back in the dark place, in the grave,
fettered to a post in the damp cellarage.

      Whereinall we differ not. But they have swept the floor,
there are no dancers, no somersaulters now,
only bricks and bleak black cement and bricks,
only the military tread and the snap of the locks.

      Mine was a threeplank bed whereon
I lay and cursed the weary sun.
They took away the prison clothes
and on the frosty nights I froze.
I had a Bible where I read
that Jesus came to raise the dead—
I kept myself from going mad
by singing an old bawdy ballad
and birds sang on my windowsill
and tortured me till I was ill,
but Archipiada came to me
and comforted my cold body
and Circe excellent utterer of her mind
lay with me in that dungeon for a year
making a silk purse from an old sow's ear
till Ronsard put a thimble on her tongue.

      Whereinall we differ not. But they have named all the stars,
trodden down the scrub of the desert, run the white moon to a schedule,
Joshua's serf whose beauty drove men mad.
They have melted the snows from Erebus, weighed the clouds,
hunted down the white bear, hunted the whale the seal the kangaroo,
they have set private enquiry agents onto Archipiada:
What is your name? Your maiden name?
Go in there to be searched. I suspect it is not your true name.
Distinguishing marks if any? (O anthropometrics!)
Now the thumbprints for filing.
Colour of hair? of eyes? of hands? O Bertillon!
How many golden prints on the smudgy page?
Homer? Adest. Dante? Adest.
Adsunt omnes, omnes et
Villon.
Villon?
Blacked by the sun, washed by the rain,
hither and thither scurrying as the wind varies.

III

Under the olive trees
walking alone
on the green terraces
very seldom
over the sea seldom
where it ravelled and spun
blue tapestries white and green
gravecloths of men
Romans and modern men
and the men of the sea
who have neither nation nor time
on the mountains seldom
the white mountains beyond
or the brown mountains between
and their drifting echoes
in the clouds and over the sea
in shrines on their ridges
the goddess of the country
silverplated in silk and embroidery
with offerings of pictures
little ships and arms
below me the ports
with naked breasts
shipless spoiled sacked
because of the beauty of Helen

precision clarifying vagueness;
boundary to a wilderness
of detail; chisel voice
smoothing the flanks of noise;
catalytic making whisper and whisper
run together like two drops of quicksilver;
factor that resolves
            unnoted harmonies;
name of the nameless;
            stuff that clings
to frigid limbs
            more marble hard
than girls imagined by Mantegna . . .

The sea has no renewal, no forgetting,
no variety of death,
is silent with the silence of a single note.

How can I sing with my love in my bosom?
Unclean, immature and unseasonable salmon.

1925

14

ATTIS: OR, SOMETHING MISSING

SONATINA

Dea magna, dea Cybele, dea domina Dindymi,
procul a mea tuus sit furor omnis, era, domo:
alios age incitatos, alios age rabidos.

I

Out of puff
noonhot in tweeds and gray felt,
tired of appearance and
disappearance;
warm obese frame limp with satiety;
slavishly circumspect at sixty;
he spreads over the ottoman
scanning the pictures and table trinkets.

(That hand's dismissed shadow
moves through fastidiously selective consciousness,
rearranges pain.)

There are no colours, words only,
and measured shaking of strings,
and flutes and oboes
enough for dancers.
. . . . reluctant ebb:
        salt from all beaches:
disrupt Atlantis, days forgotten,
extinct peoples, silted harbours.
He regrets that brackish
        train of the huntress
driven into slackening fresh,
expelled when the
        estuary resumes
colourless potability;
        wreckage that drifted
in drifts out.

"Longranked larches succeed larches, spokes of a
stroll; hounds trooping around hooves; and the stolid horn's
sweet breath. *Voice:* Have you seen the
fox? Which way did he go, he go?
There was soft rain.
I recollect deep mud and leafmould somewhere: and
in the distance Cheviot's
heatherbrown flanks and white cap.

Landscape salvaged from
evinced notice of
superabundance, of

since parsimonious
soil . . . . .

           Mother of Gods."

Mother of eunuchs.

Praise the green earth. Chance has appointed her
         home, workshop, larder, middenpit.
         Her lousy skin scabbed here and there by
         cities provides us with name and nation.

From her brooks sweat. Hers corn and fruit.
         Earthquakes are hers too. Ravenous animals
         are sent by her. Praise her and call her
         Mother and Mother of Gods and Eunuchs.

II

(*Variations on a theme by Milton*)

I thought I saw my late wife (a very respectable woman)
coming from Bywell churchyard with a handful of raisins.
I was not pleased, it is shocking to meet a ghost, so I cut her
and went and sat amongst the rank watergrasses by the Tyne.

Centrifugal tutus! Sarabands!
music clear enough to
pluck stately dances from
madness before the frenzy.
Andante . . . . *Prestissimo!*
turbulent my Orfeo!
A tumult softly hissed
as by muted violins,
Tesiphone's, Alecto's
capillary orchestra.
Long phrases falling like
intermittent private voices
suddenly in the midst of talk,
falling aslant like last light:
VENGA MEDUSA
VENGA
MEDUSA CI L'FAREM DI SMALTO
Send for Medusa: we'll enamel him!

Long loved and
too long loved, stale habit, such decay of ardour,
love never dead, love never hoping, never gay.
Ageslow venom selfsecreted. Such shame!

The gorgon's method:
         In the morning
clean streets welcomed light's renewal,

patient, passive to the weight of buses
thundering like cabinet ministers
over a lethargic populace.
Streets buffeted thin soles at midday,
streets full of beggars.
Battered, filthily unfortunate streets
perish, their ghosts are wretched
in the mockery of lamps.

And O Purveyor
of geraniums and pianos to the Kaiserin!
the hot smell of the street
conversing with the bleat
of rancid air streaming up tenement stairways!

Gods awake and fierce
stalk across the night
grasping favour of men,
power to hurt or endow,
        leave to inhabit
figure and name; or skulk
from impotence in light's
        opacity.
Day hides them, opaque day
hides their promenades; night
reveals them stalking
        (VENGA MEDUSA)
        passionately.

Polymnia
keeps a cafe in Reno.
Well, (eh, Cino?)
I dare no longer raise my eyes
on any lass
seeing what one of them has done to me.
So singlehearted, so steady
never lover, none so humble.
She made a new youth lord of her.
I lower my eyes. I say:
"I will not look on any,
maybe all are jilts."

III

Pastorale arioso
(*falsetto*)

What mournful stave, what bellow shakes the grove?
O, it is Attis grieving for his testicles!
Attis stiffening amid the snows
and the wind whining through his hair and fingers!

"Pines, my sisters, I, your sister,
chaffered for lambs in the marketplace.
I also won the 14 carat halfhunter goldwatch
at the annual sports and flowershow.
The young girls simpered when I passed.
Now I am out of a job. I would like to be lady's-maid
                    to Dindyma.

Pines, my sisters, I, your sister,
tended the bull and the entire horse.
Pensive geldings gape stale adolescence religiously,
yearning for procreative energy;
call it God. I sat amongst the atheists,
I was bankrupted by affiliation orders
who now bow my chaste vegetable forehead
                    to Dindyma.

Pines, my sisters, I, your sister,
parch in calm weather, swelter in Scirocco, sway in northwind,
I am passive to the heave of spring.
In the season I will pay my phallic harvest
                    to Dindyma.

Dindyma! Dindyma!
The wraith of my manhood,
the cruel ghost of my manhood,
                    limp in hell,
leapt sleeplessly in strange beds.
I have forgotten most of the details,
                    most of the names,
                    and the responses to
                    the ithyphallic hymns:
                    forgotten the syntax,
                    and the paradigms
grate scrappily against reluctant nerves.

(Oh Sis!
I've been 'ad!

I've been 'ad proper!)
Shall we be whole in Elysium?
I am rooted in you,
                    Dindyma!
        assure me
        the roses and myrtles,
        the lavish roses,
        the naively
        portentous myrtles,
corroborate the peacock.

(I've been 'ad!)

To whom Cybele:
  "The peacock's knavery
  keeps you in slavery.
  The roses cheat
  you, butcher's meat.
  The myrtles' pretence
  offends commonsense.
  Yet a muse defrauds
  the Mother of the Gods.
  Ponder this allegorical
  oracle."

      Attis his embleme:
      Nonnulla deest.

1931

AUS DEM ZWEITEN REICH

I

Women swarm in Tauentsienstrasse.
Clients of Nollendorferplatz cafés,
shadows on sweaty glass,
hum, drum on the table
        to the negerband's faint jazz.
Humdrum at the table.

Hour and hour
meeting against me,
efficiently whipped cream,
efficiently metropolitan chatter and snap,
transparent glistening wrapper
        for a candy pack.

Automatic, somewhat too clean,
body and soul similarly scented,
on time,
rapid, dogmatic, automatic and efficient,
ganz modern.

"Sturm über Asien" is off, some other flicker . . .
Kiss me in the taxi, twist fingers in the dark.
A box of chocolates is necessary.
I am preoccupied with Sie and Du.
        The person on the screen,
divorced and twenty-five, must pass for fourteen
for the story's sake, an insipidity
contrived to dress her in shorts
and a widenecked shirt with nothing underneath
so that you see her small breasts when she
often bends towards the camera.
Audience mainly male stirs,
        I am teased too,
I like this public blonde better than my brunette,
        but that will never do.
—Let's go,
arm in arm on foot over gleaming snow
past the Gedächtnis Kirche
to the loud crowded cafés near the Bahnhof Zoo.

Better hugged together ("to keep warm")
under street trees whimpering to the keen wind
over snow whispering to many feet,
find out a consolingly mediocre
neighborhood without music, varnished faces
bright and sagacious against varnished walls,
youngsters red from skating,

businessmen reading the papers:
no need to talk—much:
what indolence supplies.
—If, smoothing this silk skirt, you pinch my thighs,
that will be fabelhaft.

II

Herr Lignitz knows Old Berlin. It is near the Post Office
with several rather disorderly public houses.
—You have no naked pictures in your English magazines.
It is shocking. Berlin is very shocking to the English. Are you shocked?
Would you like to see the naked cabarets
in Jaegerstrasse? I think there is
nothing like that in Paris.
Or a department store? They are said to be
almost equal to Macy's in America.

III

The renowned author of
more plays than Shakespeare
stopped and did his hair
with a pocket glass
before entering the village,
afraid they wouldn't recognize
caricature and picturepostcard,
that windswept chevelure.

Who talked about poetry,
and he said nothing at all;
plays,
and he said nothing at all;
politics,
and he stirred as if a flea
bit him
but wouldn't let on in company;
and the frost in Berlin,
muttered: 𝔖𝔢𝔥𝔯𝔢𝔠𝔨𝔩𝔦𝔠𝔥.

Viennese bow from the hips,
notorieties
contorted laudatory lips,
wreaths and bouquets surround
the mindless menopause.
Stillborn fecundities,
frostbound applause.

1931

THE WELL OF LYCOPOLIS

cujus potu signa
virginitatis eripiuntur.

I   *Advis m'est que j'oy regretter*

Slinking by the jug-and-bottle
swingdoor I fell in with
Mother Venus, ageing, bedraggled, a
half-quartern of gin under her shawl,
wishing she was a young girl again:
"It's cruel hard to be getting old so soon.
I wonder I dont kill myself and have done with it.

I had them all on a string at one time,
lawyers, doctors, business-men:
there wasn't a man alive but would have given
all he possessed
for what they wont take now free for nothing.
I turned them down,
I must have had no sense,
for the sake of a shifty young fellow:
whatever I may have done at other times
on the sly
I was in love then and no mistake;
and him always knocking me about
and only cared for my money.
However much he shook me or kicked me I
loved him just the same.
If he'd made me take in washing he'd
only have had to say: 'Give us a kiss'
and I'd have forgotten my troubles.
The selfish pig, never up to any good!
He used to cuddle me. Fat lot of good it's done me!
What did I get out of it besides a bad conscience?
But he's been dead longer than thirty years
and I'm still here, old and skinny.
When I think about the old days,
what I was like and what I'm like now,
it fair drives me crazy to
look at myself with nothing on.
What a change!
Miserable dried up skin and bone.

But none of their Bacchic impertinence,
medicinal stout nor portwine-cum-beef.
A dram of anaesthetic, brother.
I'm a British subject if I *am* a colonial,
distilled liquor's clean.

It's the times have changed. I remember during the War
kids carrying the clap to school under their pinnies,
studying Belgian atrocities in the Sunday papers
or the men pissing in the backstreets; and grown women
sweating their shifts sticky at the smell of khaki
every little while.
Love's an encumberance to them who
rinse carefully before using, better
keep yourself to yourself.
What it is to be in the movement!
'Follow the instructions on page fortyone'
unlovely labour of love,
'or work it off in a day's walk,
a cold douche and brisk rub down,
there's nothing like it.'
Aye, tether me among the maniacs,
it's nicer to rave than reason."

Took her round to Polymnia's, Polymnia
glowering stedfastly at the lukewarm
undusted grate grim with cinders
never properly kindled, the brass head of the
tongs creaking as she twitched them:
'Time is, was, has been.'
A gassy fizzling spun from among the cinders.
The air, an emulsion of some unnameable oil,
greased our napes. We rhymed our breath
to the mumble of coke distilling.

"What have you come for? Why have you brought the
Goddess? You who
finger the goods you cannot purchase,
snuffle the skirt you dare not clutch.
There was never love between us, never less
than when you reckoned much. A tool
not worth the negligible price. A fool
not to be esteemed for barren honesty.
Leave me alone. A long time ago
there were men in the world, dances, guitars, ah!
Tell me, Love's mother, have I wrinkles? grey hair?
teats, or dugs? calves, or shanks?
Do I wear unbecoming garments?"

"Blotched belly, slack buttock and breast,
there's little to strip for now.
A few years makes a lot of difference.
Would you have known me?
Poor old fools,
gabbing about our young days,
squatted round a bit of fire
just lit and flickering out already:
and we used to be so pretty!"

II

May my libation of flat beer stood overnight
sour on your stomach, my devoutly worshipped ladies,
may you retch cold bile.
Windy water slurred the glint of Canopus,
am I answerable? Left, the vane
screwing perpetually ungainlywards.
What reply will a
June hailstorm countenance?

'Let's be cosy,
sit it out hand in hand.
Dreaming of you, that's all I do.'
Eiderdown air, any
girl or none, it's the same thing,
coats the tongue the morning after.
Answer?
If words were stone, if the sun's lilt
could be fixed in the stone's convexity.
Open your eyes, Polymnia,
at the sleek, slick lads treading gingerly between the bedpots,
stripped buff-naked all but their hats to raise,
and nothing rises but the hats;
smooth, with soft steps, *ambiguoque voltu*.

Daphnis investigated
bubless Chloe
behind a boulder.
Still, they say,
in another climate
virgin with virgin
coupled taste
wine without headache
and the songs are simple.
We have laid on Lycopolis water.
The nights are not fresh
between High Holborn and the Euston Road,
nor the days bright even in summer
nor the grass of the squares green.

Neither (*aequora pontis*)
on the sea's bulge
would the 'proud, full sail'
avail
us, stubborn against the trades,
closehauled,
stiff, flat canvas;
our fingers bleed
under the nail
when we reef.

III

Infamous poetry, abject love,
Aeolus' hand under her frock
this morning. This afternoon
Ocean licking her privities.
Every thrust of the autumn sun
cuckolding
in the green grin of late-flowering trees.
I shall never have anything to myself

but stare in the tank, see
Hell's constellations,
a dogstar for the Dogstar:
women's faces
blank or trivial,
still or rippled water,
a fool's image.

At my time of life it is easier not to see,
much easier to tra-la-la
a widowed tune in poor circumstances—
              tweet, tweet, twaddle,
              tweet, tweet, twat.
Squalid acquiescence in the cast-offs
of reputed poetry. Here, Bellerophon,
is a livery hack, a gelding,
easy pace, easy to hire,
all mansuetude and indifference.

Abject poetry, infamous love,
howling like a damp dog in November.
Scamped spring, squandered summer,
grain, husk, stem and stubble
mildewed; mawkish dough and sour bread.
              Tweet, tweet, twaddle. Endure
detail by detail the cunnilingual law.
"Clap a clout on your jowl for
Jesus sake! Fy for shame!
After hours, is it? or under age?
Hack off his pendants!
Can a moment of madness make up for
an age of consent?"

—with their snouts in the trough,
kecking at gummy guts,
slobbering offal, gobbling potato parings,
yellow cabbage leaves, choking on onion skin,
herring bones, slops of porridge.
Way-O! Bully boys blow!
The Gadarene swihine have got us in tow.

IV

Ed anche vo' che tu per certo credi
che sotto l'acqua ha gente che sospira.

Stuck in the mud they are saying: "We were sad
in the air, the sweet air the sun makes merry,
we were glum of ourselves, without a reason;
now we are stuck in the mud and therefore sad."
That's what they mean, but the words die in their throat;
they cannot speak out because they are stuck in the mud.
Stuck, stick, Styx. Styx, eternal, a dwelling.
But the rivers of Paradise,
the sweep of the mountains they rise in?
Drunk or daft hear
a chuckle of spring water:
drowsy suddenly wake,
but the bright peaks have faded.
Who had love for love
whose love was strong or fastidious?
Shadow and shadow noon shrinks, night shelters,
the college of Muses reconstructs
in flimsy drizzle of starlight:
bandy, hunchback, dot-and-carry-one,
praised-for-a-guinea.

Join the Royal Air Force
and See the World. The Navy will
Make a Man of You. Tour India with the Flag.
One of the ragtime army,
involuntary volunteer,
queued up for the pox in Rouen. What a blighty!
Surrendered in March. Or maybe
ulcers of mustard gas, a rivet in the lung
from scrappy shrapnel,
frostbite, trench-fever, shell-shock,
self-inflicted wound,
tetanus, malaria, influenza.
Swapped your spare boots for a packet of gaspers.
Overstayed leave.
Debauched the neighbor's little girl
to save two shillings . . .

muttering inaudibly beneath the quagmire,
irresolute, barren, dependant, this page
ripped from Love's ledger and Poetry's:
and besides I want you to know for certain
there are people under the water. They are sighing.
The surface bubbles and boils with their sighs.
Look where you will you see it.
The surface sparkles and dances with their sighs
as though Styx were silvered by a wind from Heaven.

1935

CHOMEI AT TOYAMA

(Kamo-no-Chomei, born at Kamo 1154, died at Toyama on Mount Hino, 24th June 1216)

The swirl sleeping in the waterfall!
The scum on motionless pools appearing
                    disappearing!

Eaves formal on the zenith,
lofty city Kyoto,
wealthy, without antiquities!

Housebreakers clamber about,
builders raising floor upon floor
at the corner sites, replacing
gardens by bungalows.

In the town where I was known
the young men stare at me.
A few faces I know remain.

Whence comes man at his birth? or where
does death lead him? Whom do you mourn?
Whose steps wake your delight?
Dewy hibiscus dries: though dew
outlast the petals.

I have been noting events forty years.

On the twentyseventh May eleven hundred
and seventyseven, eight p.m., fire broke out
at the corner of Tomi and Higuchi streets.
In a night
palace, ministries, university, parliament
were destroyed. As the wind veered
flames spread out in the shape of an open fan.
Tongues torn by the gusts stretched and leapt.
In the sky clouds of cinders lit red with the blaze.

Some choked, some burned, some barely escaped.
Sixteen great officials lost houses and
very many poor. A third of the city burned;
several thousands died; and of beasts,
oxen and horses and such, limitless numbers.

Men are fools to invest in real estate.

Three years less three days later a wind
starting near the outer boulevard
broke a path a quarter mile across
to Sixth Avenue.

Not a house stood. Some were felled whole,
some in splinters; some had left
great beams upright in the ground
and round about
lay rooves scattered where the wind flung them.
Flocks of furniture in the air,
everything flat fluttered like dead leaves.
A dust like fog or smoke,
you could hear nothing for the roar,
                    "bufera infernal!"
Lamed some, wounded some.
This cyclone turned southwest.

Massacre without cause.

Portent?

The same year thunderbolted change of capital,
fixed here, Kyoto, for ages.
Nothing compelled the change nor was it an easy matter
but the grumbling was disproportionate.
We moved, those with jobs
or wanting jobs or hangers on of the rest,
in haste haste fretting to be the first.
Rooftrees overhanging empty rooms;
dismounted: floating down the river;
The soil returned to heath.

I visited the new site: narrow and too uneven,
cliffs and marshes, deafening shores, perpetual strong winds;
the palace a logcabin dumped amongst the hills
(yet not altogether inelegant).
There was no flat place for houses, many vacant lots,
the former capital wrecked, the new a camp,
and thoughts like clouds changing, frayed by a breath:
peasants bewailing lost land, newcomers aghast at prices.
No one in uniform: the crowds
resembled demobilized conscripts.

There were murmurs. Time defined them.
In the winter the decree was rescinded,
we returned to Kyoto;
but the houses were gone and none
could afford to rebuild them.

I have heard of a time when kings beneath bark rooves
watched the chimneys.
When smoke was scarce, taxes were remitted.

To appreciate present conditions
collate them with those of antiquity.

Drought, floods, and a dearth. Two fruitless autumns.

Empty markets, swarms of beggars. Jewels
sold for a handful of rice. Dead stank
on the curb, lay so thick on
Riverside Drive a car couldn't pass.
The pest bred.
That winter my fuel was the walls of my own house.

Fathers fed their children and died,
babies died sucking the dead.
The priest Hoshi went about marking their foreheads
A, Amida, their requiem;
he counted them in the East End in the last two months,
fortythree thousand A's.

Crack, rush, ye mountains, bury your rills!
Spread your green glass, ocean, over the meadows!
Scream, avalanche, boulders amok, strangle the dale!
O ships in the sea's power, O horses
on shifting roads, in the earth's power, without hoofhold!
This is the earthquake, this was
the great earthquake of Genryaku!

The chapel fell, the abbey, the minister and the small shrines
fell, their dust rose and a thunder of houses falling.
O to be birds and fly or dragons and ride on a cloud!
The earthquake, the great earthquake of Genryaku!

A child building a mud house against a high wall:
I saw him crushed suddenly, his eyes hung
from their orbits like two tassels.
His father howled shamelessly—an officer.
I was not abashed at his crying.

Such shocks continued three weeks; then lessening,
but still a score daily as big as an average earthquake;
then fewer, alternate days, a tertian ague of tremors.
There is no record of any greater.
It caused a religious revival.
Months . . .
Years . . .
. . . .
Nobody mentions it now.

This is the unstable world and
we in it unstable and our houses.

The poor man living amongst the rich
gives no rowdy parties, doesn't sing.
Dare he keep his child at home, keep a dog?
He dare not pity himself above a whimper.

But he visits, he flatters, he is put in his place,
he remembers the patch on his trousers.
His wife and sons despise him for being poor.
He has no peace.

If he lives in an alley of rotting frame houses
he dreads a fire.
If he commutes he loses his time
and leaves his house daily to be plundered by gunmen.

The bureaucrats are avaricious.
He who has no relatives in the Inland Revenue,
poor devil!

Whoever helps him enslaves him
and follows him crying out: *"Gratitude!"*
If he wants success he is wretched.
If he doesn't he passes for mad.

Where shall I settle, what trade choose
that the mind may practise, the body rest?

My grandmother left me a house
but I was always away
for my health and because I was alone there.
When I was thirty I couldn't stand it any longer,
I built a house to suit myself:
one bamboo room, you would have thought it was a cartshed,
poor shelter from snow or wind.
It stood on the flood plain. And that quarter
is also flooded with gangsters.

One generation
I saddened myself with idealistic philosophies,
but before I was fifty
I perceived that there was no time to lose,
left home and conversation.
Among the cloudy mountains of Ohara
spring and autumn, spring and autumn, spring and autumn,
emptier than ever.

The dew evaporates from my sixty years,
I have built my last house, or hovel,
a hunter's bivouac, an old
silkworm's cocoon:
ten feet by ten, seven high: and I,
reckoning it a lodging not a dwelling,
omitted the usual foundation ceremony.

I have filled the frames with clay,
set hinges at the corners;
easy to take it down and carry it away
when I get bored with this place.

Two barrowloads of junk
and the cost of a man to shove the barrow,
no trouble at all.

Since I have trodden Hino mountain
noon has beaten through the awning
over my bamboo balcony, evening
shone on Amida.
I have shelved my books above the window,
lute and mandolin near at hand,
piled bracken and a little straw for bedding,
a smooth desk where the light falls, stove for bramblewood.
I have gathered stones, fitted
stones for a cistern, laid bamboo
pipes. No woodstack,
wood enough in the thicket.

Toyama, snug in the creepers!
Toyama, deep in the dense gully, open
westward whence the dead ride out of Eden
squatting on blue clouds of wistaria.
(Its scent drifts west to Amida.)

Summer? Cuckoo's *Follow, follow*—to
harvest Purgatory hill!
Fall? The nightgrasshopper will
shrill *Fickle life*!
Snow will thicken on the doorstep,
melt like a drift of sins.
No friend to break silence,
no one will be shocked if I neglect the rite.
There's a Lent of commandments kept
where there's no way to break them.

A ripple of white water after a boat,
shining water after the boats Mansami saw
rowing at daybreak
at Okinoya.
"Between the maple leaf and the caneflower"
murmurs the afternoon—Po Lo-tien
saying goodbye on the verge of Jinyo river.
(I am playing scales on my mandolin.)

Be limber, my fingers, I am going to play "Autumn Wind"
to the pines, I am going to play "Hastening Brook"
to the water. I am no player
but there's nobody listening,
I do it for my own amusement.

Sixteen and sixty, I and the gamekeeper's boy,
one zest and equal, chewing tsubana buds,
one zest and equal, persimmon, pricklypear,
ears of sweetcorn pilfered from Valley Farm.

The view from the summit: sky bent over Kyoto,
picnic villages, Fushimi and Toba:
a very economical way of enjoying yourself.
Thought runs along the crest, climbs Sumiyama;
beyond Kasatori it visits the great church,
goes on pilgrimage to Ishiyama (no need to foot it!)
or the graves of poets, of Semimaru who said:
> *"Somehow or other*
> *we scuttle through a lifetime.*
> *Somehow or other*
> *neither palace nor straw-hut*
> *is quite satisfactory."*

Not emptyhanded, with cherryblossom, with red maple
as the season gives it to decorate my Buddha
or offer a sprig at a time to chancecomers, home!

A fine moonlit night,
I sit at the window with a headful of old verses.

"Whenever a monkey howls there are tears on my cuff."

"Those are fireflies that seem
the fishermen's lights
off Maki island."

A shower at dawn
sings
like the hillbreeze in the leaves.

"At the pheasant's chirr I recall
my father and mother uncertainly."

I rake my ashes.

> *"Chattering fire,*
soon kindled, soon burned out,
fit wife for an old man!"

Neither closed in one landscape
nor in one season
the mind moving in illimitable
recollection.

I came here for a month
five years ago.
There's moss on the roof.

And I hear Soanso's dead
back in Kyoto.
I have as much room as I need.

I know myself and mankind.
. . . .
I don't want to be bothered.

(You will make me editor
of the Imperial Anthology?

I don't want to be bothered.)

You build for your wife, children,
cousins and cousins' cousins.
You want a house to entertain in.

A man like me can have neither servants nor friends
in the present state of society.
If I did not build for myself
for whom should I build?

Friends fancy a rich man's riches,
friends suck up to a man in high office.
If you keep straight you will have no friends
but catgut and blossom in season.

Servants weigh out their devotion
in proportion to their perquisites.
What do they care for peace and quiet?
There are more pickings in town.

I sweep my own floor
—less fuss.
I walk; I get tired
but do not have to worry about a horse.

My hands and feet will not loiter
when I am not looking.
I will not overwork them.
Besides, it's good for the health.

My jacket's wistaria flax,
my blanket hemp,
berries and young greens
my food.

(Let it be quite understood,
all this is merely personal.
I am not preaching the simple life
to those who enjoy being rich.)

I am shifting rivermist, not to be trusted.
I do not ask anything extraordinary of myself.
I like a nap after dinner
and to see the seasons come round in good order.

Hankering, vexation and apathy,
that's the run of the world.
Hankering, vexation and apathy,
keeping a carriage wont cure it.

Keeping a man in livery
wont cure it. Keeping a private fortress
wont cure it. These things satisfy no craving.
Hankering, vexation and apathy . . .

I am out of place in the capital,
people take me for a beggar,
as you would be out of place in this sort of life,
you are so—I regret it—so welded to your vulgarity.

The moonshadow merges with darkness
on the cliffpath,
a tricky turn near ahead.

Oh! There's nothing to complain about.
Buddha says: "None of the world is good".
I am fond of my hut . . .

I have renounced the world;
have a saintly
appearance.

I do not enjoy being poor,
I've a passionate nature.
My tongue
clacked a few prayers.

1932

ODES

1

Weeping oaks grieve, chestnuts raise
mournful candles. Sad is spring
to perpetuate, sad to trace
immortalities never changing.

Weary on the sea
for sight of land
gazing past the coming wave we
see the same wave;

drift on merciless reiteration of years;
descry no death; but spring
is everlasting
resurrection.

1924

2

Farewell ye sequent graces
voided faces still evasive!
Silent leavetaking and mournful
as nightwanderings
in unlit rooms or where the glow
of wall-reflected streetlamp light
or hasty matches shadowed large
and crowded out by imps of night
glimmer on cascades of
phantom dancers.
Airlapped, silent muses of Light,
cease to administer
poisons to dying memories to stir
pangs of old rapture, cease to conspire
reunions of inevitable seed
long blown barren sown gathered
haphazard to wither.

1924

I am agog for foam. Tumultuous come
with teeming sweetness to the bitter shore
tidelong unrinsed and midday parched and numb
with expectation. If the bright sky bore
with endless utterance of a single blue
unphrased, its restless immobility
infects the soul, which must decline into
an anguished and exact sterility
and waste away: then how much more the sea
trembling with alteration must perfect
our loneliness by its hostility.
The dear companionship of its elect
deepens our envy. Its indifference
haunts us to suicide. Strong memories
of sprayblown days exasperate impatience
to brief rebellion and emphasise
the casual impotence we sicken of.
But when mad waves spring, braceletted with foam,
towards us in the angriness of love
crying a strange name, tossing as they come
repeated invitations in the gay
exuberance of unexplained desire,
we can forget the sad splendour and play
at wilfulness until the gods require
renewed inevitable hopeless calm
and the foam dies and we again subside
into our catalepsy, dreaming foam,
while the dry shore awaits another tide.

1926

4

After the grimaces of capitulation
the universal face resumes its cunning, quick
to abandon the nocturnal elevation.
                    In repose majestic,
vile wakening, cowering under its tyrant
eager in stratagems to circumvent the harsh
performer of unveilings, revealer of gaunt
lurking anatomy, grin of diurnal farce;
yet when the fellow with the red-hot poker comes
truculently to torment our blisters, we vie
with one another to present scarified bums
to the iron, clutching sausages greedily.
O Sun! Should I invoke this scorn, participate
in the inconsequence of this defeat, or hide
in noctambulistic exile to penetrate
secrets that moon and stars and empty death deride?

1926

5   *To Helen Egli*

Empty vast days built in the waste memory seem a jail for
thoughts grown stale in the mind, tardy of birth, rank and inflexible:
love and slow selfpraise, even grief's cogency, all emotions
timetamed whimper and shame changes the past brought to no utterance.

Ten or ten thousand, does it much signify, Helen, how we
date fantasmal events, London or Troy? Let Polyhymnia
strong with cadence multiply song, voices enmeshed by music
respond bringing the savour of our sadness or delight again.

1927

6   *Personal Column*

. . .As to my heart, that may as well be forgotten
or labelled: Owner will dispose of same
to a good home, refs. exchgd., h. & c.,
previous experience desired but not essential
or let on a short lease to suit convenience.

1927

7

The day being Whitsun we had pigeon for dinner;
but Richmond in the pitted river saw
mudmirrored mackintosh, a wet southwest
wiped and smeared dampness over Twickenham.

Pools on the bustop's buttoned tarpaulin.
Wimbledon, Wandsworth, Clapham, the Oval. "Lo,
Westminster Palace where the asses jaw!"

Endless disappointed buckshee-hunt!
Suburb and city giftless garden and street,
and the sky alight of an evening stubborn
and mute by day and never *rei novae*
inter rudes artium homines.
                never a spark of sedition
amongst the uneducated workingmen.

1928

8   *Each fettered ghost slips to his several grave.*

Loud intolerant bells (the shrinking nightflower closes
tenderly round its stars to baulk their hectoring)
orate to deaf hills where the olive stirs and dozes
in easeless age, dim to farce of man's fashioning.

Shepherd's away! They toll throngs to your solitude
and their inquisitive harangue will disembody
shames and delights, all private features of your mood,
flay out your latencies, sieve your hopes, fray your shoddy.

The distant gods enorbed in bright indifference
whom we confess creatures or abstracts of our spirit,
unadored, absorbed into the incoherence,
leave dessicated names: rabbits sucked by a ferret.

1928

9

Dear be still! Time's start of us lengthens slowly.
Bright round plentiful nights ripen and fall for us.
Those impatient thighs will be bruised soon enough.

Sniff the sweet narcotic distilled by coupled
skins; moist bodies relaxed, mild, unemotional.
Thrifty fools spoil love with their headlong desires.

Dally! Waste! Mock! Loll! till the chosen sloth fails,
huge gasps empty the loins shuddering chilly in
long accumulated delight's thunderstorm.

Rinsed in cool sleep day will renew the summer
lightnings. Leave it to me. Only a savage's
lusts explode slapbang at the first touch like bombs.

1929

10 CHORUS OF FURIES   *Guarda mi disse, le feroce Erine*

Let us come upon him first as if in a dream,
anonymous triple presence,
memory made substance and tally of heart's rot:
then in the waking Now be demonstrable, seem
sole aspect of being's essence,
coffin to the living touch, self's Iscariot.
Then he will loath the year's recurrent long caress
without hope of divorce,
envying idiocy's apathy or the stress
of definite remorse.
He will lapse into a halflife lest the taut force
of the mind's eagerness
recall those fiends or new apparitions endorse
his excessive distress.
He will shrink, his manhood leave him, slough selfaware
the last skin of the flayed: despair.
He will nurse his terror carefully, uncertain
even of death's solace,
impotent to outpace
dispersion of the soul, disruption of the brain.

1929

Narciss, my numerous cancellations prefer
slow limpness in the damp dustbins amongst the peel
tobacco-ash and ends spittoon lickings litter
of labels dry corks breakages and a great deal

of miscellaneous garbage picked over by
covetous dustmen and Salvation Army sneaks
to one review-rid month's printed ignominy,
the public detection of your decay, that reeks.

1929

12

An arles, an arles for my hiring,
O master of singers, an arlespenny!

—Well sung singer, said Apollo,
but in this trade we pay no wages.

I too was once a millionaire
(in Germany during the inflation:
when the train steamed into Holland
I had not enough for a bun.)

The Lady asked the Poet:
Why do you wear your raincoat in the drawing-room?
He answered: Not to show
my arse sticking out of my trousers.

His muse left him for a steady man.
Quaeret in trivio vocationem.

(he is cadging for drinks at the streetcorners.)

1929

Muzzle and jowl and beastly brow,
bilious glaring eyes, tufted ears,
recidivous criminality in the slouch,
—This is not the latest absconding bankrupt
but a 'beautiful' tiger imported at great expense from
Kuala Lumpur.

7 photographers, 4 black-and-white artists and an R.A.
are taking his profitable likeness;
28 reporters and an essayist
are writing him up.
Sundry ladies think he is a darling
especially at mealtimes, observing
that a firm near the Docks advertises replicas
fullgrown on approval for easy cash payments.

♂Felis Tigris (Straits Settlements) (Bobo) takes exercise
up and down his cage before feeding
in a stench of excrements of great cats
indifferent to beauty or brutality.
He is said to have eaten several persons
but of course you can never be quite sure of these things.

1929

14   GIN THE GOODWIFE STINT

The ploughland has gone to bent
and the pasture to heather;
gin the goodwife stint,
she'll keep the house together.

Gin the goodwife stint
and the bairns hunger
the Duke can get his rent
one year longer.

The Duke can get his rent
and we can get our ticket
twa pund emigrant
on a C.P.R. packet.

1930

15

Nothing
substance utters or time
stills and restrains
joins the design and the

supple measure deftly
as thought's intricate polyphonic
score dovetails with the tread
sensuous things
keep in our consciousness.

Celebrate man's craft
and the word spoken in shapeless night, the
sharp tool paring away
waste and the forms
cut out of mystery!

When the taut string's note
passes ears' reach or red rays or violet
fade, strong over unseen
forces the word
ranks and enumerates . . .

mimes the clouds condensed
and the hewn hills and the bristling forests,
steadfast corn in its season
and the seasons
in their due array,

life of man's own body
and death . . .
            The sound thins into melody,
discourse narrowing, craft
failing, design
petering out.

Ears heavy to breeze of speech and
thud of the ictus.

1930

16

Molten pool, incandescent spilth of
deep cauldrons—and brighter nothing is—
cast and cold, your blazes extinct and
no turmoil nor peril left you,
rusty ingot, bleak paralysed blob!

1930

17

Now that sea's over that island
so that barely on a calm day sun sleeks
a patchwork hatching of combed weed
over stubble and fallow alike
I resent drowned blackthorn hedge, choked ditch,
gates breaking from rusty hinges,
the submerged copse,
"Trespassers will be prosecuted."

Sea's over that island,
weed over furrow and dungheap:
but how I should recognise the place
under the weeds and sand
who was never in it on land I don't know:
some trick of refraction,
a film of light in the water crumpled and spread
like a luminous frock on a woman walking
alone in her garden.

Oval face, thin eyebrows wide of the eyes,
a premonition in the gait
of this subaqueous persistence
of a particular year—
for you had prepared it for preservation
not vindictively, urged
by the economy of passions.

Nobody said: She is organising
these knicknacks her dislike collects
into a pattern nature will adopt and perpetuate.

Weed over meadowgrass, sea over weed,
no step on the gravel.
Very likely I shall never meet her again
or if I do, fear the latch as before.

1930

On the up-platform at Morpeth station
in the market-day throng
I overheard a Morpethshire farmer
muttering this song:

Must ye bide, my good stone house,
to keep a townsman dry?
To hear the flurry of the grouse
but not the lowing of the kye?

To see the bracken choke the clod
the coulter will na turn?
The bit level neebody
will drain soak up the burn?

Where are ye, my seven score sheep?
Feeding on other braes!
My brand has faded from your fleece,
another has its place.

The fold beneath the rowan
where ye were dipt before,
its cowpit walls are overgrown,
ye would na heed them more.

And thou! Thou's idled all the spring,
I doubt thou's spoiled, my Meg!
But a sheepdog's faith is aye something.
We'll hire together in Winnipeg.

Canada's a cold land.
Thou and I must share
a straw bed and a hind's wages
and the bitter air.

Canada's a bare land
for the north wind and the snow.
Northumberland's a bare land
for men have made it so.

Sheep and cattle are poor men's food,
grouse is sport for the rich;
heather grows where the sweet grass might grow
for the cost of cleaning the ditch.

A liner lying in the Clyde
will take me to Quebec.
My sons'll see the land I am leaving
as barren as her deck.

1930

19

Fruits breaking the branches,
sunlight stagnates in the rift;
here the curl of a comma,
parenthesis,

(Put the verb out of mind, lurking
to jar all to a period!)
discourse interminably
uncontradicted

level under the orchards'
livid-drowsy green:
this that Elysium
they speak of.

Where shall I hide?

1930

20   VESTIGES

I

Salt grass silent of hooves, the lake stinks,
we take a few small fish from the streams,
our children are scabby, chivvied by flies,
we cannot read the tombs in the eastern prairie,
        who slew the Franks, who
        swam the Yellow River.

The lice have left Temuchin's tent. His ghost
cries under north wind, having spent
strength in life: life lost, lacks means of death,
voice-tost; the horde indistinguishable;
worn name weak in fool's jaws.

We built no temples. Our cities' woven hair
mildewed and frayed. Records of Islam and Chin,
battles, swift riders, the ambush,
tale of the slain, and the name Jengiz.

Wild geese of Yen, peacocks of the Windy Shore.

Tall Chutsai sat under the phoenix tree.
—That Baghdad banker contracts to
double the revenue, him collecting.

Four times might be exacted, but
such taxation impoverishes the people.

No litigation. The laws were simple.

II

Jengiz to Chang Chun: China
is fat, but I am lean
eating soldier's food,
lacking learning.
In seven years
I brought most of the world under one law.
The Lords of Cathay
hesitate and fall.
Amidst these disorders
I distrust my talents.
To cross a river
boats and rudders,
to keep the empire in order
poets and sages,
but I have not found nine for a cabinet,
not three.
I have fasted and washed. Come.

Chang: I am old
not wise nor virtuous,
nor likely to be much use.
My appearance is parched, my body weak.
I set out at once.

And to Liu Chung Lu, Jengiz:
Get an escort and a good cart,
and the girls can be sent on
separately if he insists.

1931

21 TWO PHOTOGRAPHS

It's true then that you still overeat, fat friend,
and swell, and never take folk's advice. They laugh,
you just giggle and pay no attention. Damn!
               you don't care, not you!

But once—that was before time had blunted your
desire for pretty frocks—slender girl—or is
the print cunningly faked?—arm in arm with your
               fiancé you stood

and glared into the lens (slightly out of focus)
while that public eye scrutinised your shape,
afraid, the attitude shows, you might somehow
               excite its dislike.

1932

22

Mesh cast for mackerel
by guess and the sheen's tremor,
imperceptible if you haven't the knack—
a difficult job,

hazardous and seasonal:
many shoals all of a sudden,
it would tax the Apostles to take the lot;
then drowse for months,

nets on the shingle,
a pint in the tap.
Likewise the pilchards come unexpectedly,
startle the man on the cliff.

Remember us to the teashop girls.
Say we have seen no legs better than theirs,
we have the sea to stare at,
its treason, copiousness, tedium.

1932

23 THE PASSPORT OFFICER

This impartial dog's nose
scrutinizes the lamppost. All in good order.
He sets his seal on it and
moves on to the next.

(The drippings of his forerunners
convey no information,
barely a precedent.
His actions are reflex.)

1932

24

Vessels thrown awry by strong gusts
broach too, the seas capsize them.
Sundry cargoes have
strewn the gulf with flotsam
in parcels too small to be salvaged.

     (In the purlieus? or the precincts?
     Lord Shaw had it argued
     a week in the Lords:
     a guinea a minute
     more or less.)

Some attribute the series of wrecks hereabouts to
faulty stowage, an illfound ship,
careless navigation or the notorious reefs,
just awash at low tide.
The place has a bad name.

     (Stern in the purlieus, bow in the precincts,
     the mate in the purlieus,
     the chief engineer
     together with the donkeyman
     at that moment in the precincts.)

Nevertheless we have heard
voices speech eludes allude to
gales not measured by the anemometer
nor predicted in Kingsway.
They defy Epicurus.

(Lord Shaw quoted Solomon,
advised a compromise.
Lord Carson muttered
'Purlieus or precincts
the place has a bad name.')

Here was glass-clear architecture,
gardens sacred to Tethys.

Ocean spare the new twinscrew dieselengined tanker,
spare the owners and underwriters
litigation.

1933

25

As appleblossom to crocus
typist to cottage lass,
perishable alike, unlike
the middleclass rose.

Each sour noon
squeezed into teashops
displays one at least
delicate ignorant face

untroubled by
earth's spinning,
preoccupied rather
by the set of her stocking.

Men are timid,
hotels expensive,
the police keep
a sharp eye on landladies.

—The cinema, Postume,
Postume, warm,
in the old days
before thirty.

1934

26

Two hundred and seven paces
        from the tram-stop
to the door,

a hundred and forty-six thousand
        four hundred
seconds ago,

two hundred and ninety-two thousand
        eight hundred
kisses or thereabouts; what else

let him say who saw and let
        him who is able
do like it for I'm

not fit for a commonplace world
        any longer I'm
bound for the City,

cashregister, adding-machine,
        rotary stencil.
Give me another

double whiskey and fire-extinguisher,
        George. Here's
Girls! Girls!

1934

27

On highest summits dawn comes soonest
(But that is not the time to give over loving.)

1935

28

You leave
nobody else
without a bed

you make
everybody else
thoroughly at home

I'm
the only one
hanged
in your
halter

you've driven
nobody else mad
but me.

1935

29

Southwind, tell her what
won't sadden her,
not how wretched
I am.

Do you sleep snug these
long nights or
know I am lying
alone?

1935

Four white heifers with sprawling hooves
          trundle the waggon.
     Its ill-roped crates heavy with fruit sway.
The chisel point of the goad, blue and white,
          glitters ahead,
     a flame to follow lance-high in a man's hand
who does not shave. His linen trousers
          like him want washing.
     You can see his baked skin through his shirt.
He has no shoes and his hat has a hole in it.
          "Hu! vaca! Hu! vaca!"
     he says staccato without raising his voice;
"Adios caballero" legato but
          in the same tone.
     Camelmen high on muzzled mounts
boots rattling against the panels
          of an empty
     packsaddle do not answer strangers.
Each with his train of seven or eight tied
          head to tail they
     pass silent but for the heavy bells
and plip of slobber dripping from
          muzzle to dust;
     save that on sand their soles squeak slightly.
Milkmaids, friendly girls between
          fourteen and twenty
     or younger, bolt upright on small
trotting donkeys that bray (they arch their
          tails a few inches
     from the root, stretch neck and jaw forward
to make the windpipe a trumpet)
          chatter. Jolted
     cans clatter. The girls' smiles repeat
the black silk curve of the wimple
          under the chin.
     Their hats are absurd doll's hats
or flat-crowned to take a load.
          All have fine eyes.
     You can guess their balanced nakedness
under the cotton gown and thin shift.
          They sing and laugh.
     They say "Adios!" shyly but look back
more than once, knowing our thoughts
          and sharing our
     desires and lack of faith in desire.

1935

The soil sandy and the plow light, neither
virgin land nor near by the market town,
cropping one staple without forethought, steer
stedfastly ruinward year in year out,
grudging the labour and cost of manure,
drudging not for gain but fewer dollars loss
yet certain to make a bad bargain by
misjudging the run of prices. How glad
you will be when the state takes your farm for
arrears of taxes! No more cold daybreaks
saffron under the barbed wire the east wind
thrums, nor wet noons, nor starpinned nights! The choir
of gnats is near a full-close. The windward
copse stops muttering inwardly its prose
bucolics. You will find a city job
or relief—or doss-and-grub—resigned to
anything except your own numb toil, the
seasonal plod to spoil the land, alone.

1936

32

Let them remember Samangan, the bridge and tower
and rutted cobbles and the coppersmith's hammer,
where we looked out from the walls to the marble mountains
ate and lay and were happy an hour and a night;

so that the heart never rests from love of the city
without lies or riches, whose old women
straight as girls at the well are beautiful,
its old men and its wineshops gay.

Let them remember Samangan against usurers,
cheats and cheapjacks, amongst boasters,
hideous children of cautious marriages,
those who drink in contempt of joy.

Let them remember Samangan, remember
they wept to remember the hour and go.

1937

To Anne de Silver

I

Not to thank dogwood nor
the wind that sifts
petals are these words,
nor for a record,

but, as notes sung and received
still the air,
these are controlled by
yesterday evening,

a peal after
the bells have rested.

II

Lest its meaning
escape the dogwood's
whiteness, these:

Days now
less bitter than
rind of wild gourd.
Cool breezes. Lips
moistened, there are words.

1938

To Violet, with prewar poems.

These tracings from a world that's dead
take for my dust-smothered pyramid.
Count the sharp study and long toil
as pavements laid for worms to soil.
You without knowing it might tread
the grass where my foundation's laid,
you, or another's, house be built
where my weathered stones lie spilt,
and this unread memento be
the only lasting part of me.

1941

35

Search under every veil
for the pale eyes, pale
lips of a sick child,
in each doorway glimpse
her reluctant limbs
for whom no kindness is,
to whom caress and kiss
come nightly more amiss,
whose hand no gentle hand
touches, whose eyes withstand
compassion. Say: Done, past
help, preordained waste.
Say: We know by the dead
they mourn, their bloodshed,
the maimed who are the free.
We willed it, we.
Say: Who am I to doubt?
But every vein cries out.

1947

36

See! Their verses are laid
as mosaic gold to gold
gold to lapis lazuli
white marble to porphyry
stone shouldering stone, the dice
polished alike, there is
no cement seen and no gap
between stones as the frieze strides
to the impending apse:
the rays of many glories
forced to its focus forming
a glory neither of stone
nor metal, neither of words
nor verses, but of the light
shining upon no substance:
a glory not made
for which all else was made.

1948

There are the Alps. What is there to say about them?
They dont make sense. Fatal glaciers, crags cranks climb,
jumbled boulder and weed, pasture and boulder, scree,
et l'on entend, maybe, *le refrain joyeux et leger*.
Who knows what the ice will have scraped on the rock it is smoothing?

There they are, you will have to go a long way round
if you want to avoid them.
It takes some getting used to. There are the Alps,
fools! Sit down and wait for them to crumble!

1949

OVERDRAFTS

Darling of Gods and Men, beneath the gliding stars
you fill rich earth and buoyant sea with your presence
for every living thing achieves its life through you,
rises and sees the sun. For you the sky is clear,
the tempests still. Deft earth scatters her gentle flowers,
the level ocean laughs, the softened heavens glow
with generous light for you. In the first days of spring
when the untrammelled allrenewing southwind blows
the birds exult in you and herald your coming.
Then the shy cattle leap and swim the brooks for love.
Everywhere, through all seas mountains and waterfalls,
love caresses all hearts and kindles all creatures
to overmastering lust and ordained renewals.
Therefore, since you alone control the sum of things
and nothing without you comes forth into the light
and nothing beautiful or glorious can be
without you, Alma Venus! trim my poetry
with your grace; and give peace to write and read and think.

(Lucretius)

1927

Yes, it's slow, docked of amours,
      docked of the doubtless efficacious
bottled makeshift, gin; but who'd risk being bored stiff
every night listening to father's silly sarcasms?

If your workbox is mislaid
      blame Cytherea's lad . . . Minerva
's not at all pleased that your seam's dropped for a fair
                                    sight
of that goodlooking athlete's glistening wet shoulders

when he's been swimming and stands
      towelling himself in full view
of the house. Ah! but you should see him on horseback!
or in track-shorts! He's a first-class middleweight pug.

He can shoot straight from the butts,
      straight from precarious cover, waistdeep
in the damp sedge, having stayed motionless daylong
when the driven tiger appears suddenly at arms'-length.

(Horace)

1931

Please stop gushing about his pink
neck smooth arms and so forth, Dulcie; it makes me sick,
badtempered, silly: makes me blush.
Dribbling sweat on my chops proves I'm on tenterhooks.
—White skin bruised in a boozing bout,
ungovernable cub certain to bite out a
permanent memorandum on
those lips. Take my advice, better not count on your
tough guy's mumbling your pretty mouth
always. Only the thrice blest are in love for life,
we others are divorced at heart
soon, soon torn apart by wretched bickerings.

(Horace)

1931

VERSE AND VERSION

In that this happening
        is not unkind
it put to
        shame every kindness

mind, mouths, their words,
        people, put sorrow
                on
        its body

before sorrow it came
        and before every kindness,
happening for every sorrow
        before every kindness

(Louis Zukofsky)

quia id quod accidit
        non est immitis
pudebat omnia
        mitiora.

mens, ora, dicta horum,
        hominesque, tristitiam
superimponunt
        eius membra.

prius quam tristitia accidit,
        omnisque prius quam mitiora;
accidit pro omnibus tristitiis
        prius quam omnia mitiora.

(Basil Bunting)

1932

When the sword of sixty comes nigh his head
give a man no wine, for he is drunk with years.
Age claps a stick in my bridle-hand:
substance spent, health broken,
forgotten the skill to swerve aside from the joust
with the spearhead grazing my eyelashes.

The sentinel perched on the hill top
cannot see the countless army he used to see there:
the black summit's deep in snow
and its lord himself sinning against the army.

He was proud of his two swift couriers:
lo! sixty ruffians have put them in chains.
The singer is weary of his broken voice,
one drone for the bulbul alike and the lion's grousing.

Alas for flowery, musky, sappy thirty
and the sharp Persian sword!
The pheasant strutting about the briar,
pomegranate-blossom and cypress sprig!
Since I raised my glass to fifty-eight
I have toasted only the bier and the burial ground.

I ask the just Creator
so much refuge from Time
that a tale of mine may remain in the world
from this famous book of the ancients
and they who speak of such matters weighing their words
think of that only when they think of me.

(Firdosi)

1935

Abu'abdulla Ja'far bin Mahmud Rudaki of Samarkand says:

All the teeth ever I had are worn down and fallen out.
They were not rotten teeth, they shone like a lamp,
a row of silvery-white pearls set in coral;
they were as the morning star and as drops of rain.
There are none left now, all of them wore out and fell out.
Was it ill-luck, ill-luck, a malign conjunction?
It was no fault of stars, nor yet length of years.
I will tell you what it was: it was God's decree.

The world is always like a round, rolling eye,
round and rolling since it existed: a cure for pain
and then again a pain that supplants the cure.
In a certain time it makes new things old,
in a certain time makes new what was worn threadbare.
Many a broken desert has been gay garden,
many gay gardens grow where there used to be desert.

What can you know, my blackhaired beauty,
what I was like in the old days?
You tickle your lover with your curls
but never knew the time when he had curls.
The days are past when his face was good to look on,
the days are past when his hair was jet black.
Likewise, comeliness of guests and friends was dear,
but one dear guest will never return.
Many a beauty may you have marvelled at
but I was always marvelling at her beauty.
The days are past when she was glad and gay
and overflowing with mirth and I was afraid of losing her.
He paid, your lover, well and in counted coin
in any town where was a girl with round hard breasts,
and plenty of good girls had a fancy for him
and came by night but by day dare not
for dread of the husband and the jail.

Bright wine and the sight of a gracious face
dear it might cost, but always cheap to me.
My purse was my heart, my heart bursting with words,
and the title-page of my book was Love and Poetry.
Happy was I, not understanding grief,
any more than a meadow.
Silk-soft has poetry made many a heart
stone before and heavy as an anvil.

Eyes turned always towards little nimble curls,
ears turned always towards men wise in words,
neither household, wife, child nor a patron—
at ease of these trials and at rest!
Oh! my dear, you look at Rudaki
but never saw him in the days when he was like that.

Never saw him when he used to go about
singing his songs as though he had a thousand.
The days are past when bold men sought his company,
the days are past when he managed affairs of princes,
the days are past when all wrote down his verses,
the days are past when he was the Poet of Khorassan.

Wherever there was a gentleman of renown
in his house had I silver and a mount.
From whomsoever some had greatness and gifts,
greatness and gifts had I from the house of Saman.
The Prince of Khorassan gave me forty thousand dirhems,
Prince Makan more by a fifth,
and eight thousand in all from his nobles
severally. That was the fine time!
When the Prince heard a fair phrase he gave, and his men,
each man of his nobles, as much as the Prince saw fit.
Times have changed. I have changed. Bring me my stick.
Now for the beggar's staff and wallet.

(Rudaki)

1948

Shall I sulk because my love has a double heart?
Happy is he whose she is singlehearted!
She has found me a new torment for every instant
and I am, whatever she does, content, content.
If she has bleached my cheek with her love, say: Bleach!
Is not pale saffron prized above poppy red?
If she has stooped my shoulders, say to them: Stoop!
Must not a harp be bent when they string it to sing?
If she has kindled fire in my heart, say: Kindle!
Only a kindled candle sends forth light.
If tears rain from my eyes, say: Let them rain!
Spring rains make fair gardens. And if then
she has cast me into the shadow of exile, say:
Those who seek fortune afar find it the first.

(from a qasida of Manuchehri)

1949

Came to me—
      Who?
She.
      When?
In the dawn, afraid.

      What of?
Anger.
      Whose?
Her father's.
      Confide!

I kissed her twice.
      Where?
On her moist mouth.
      Mouth?

No.
      What, then?
Cornelian.
      How was it?
Sweet.

(Rudaki)

1949

This I write, mix ink with tears,
and have written of grief before, but never so grievously,
to tell Azra Vamiq's pain,
to tell Laila Majnun's plight,
to tell you my own
unfinished story.
Take it. Seek no excuse.
How sweetly you will sing what I so sadly write.

(attributed, probably wrongly, to Sa'di)

1949

Last night without sight of you my brain was ablaze.
My tears trickled and fell plip on the ground. That I with
sighing might bring my life to a close they would name
you and again and again speak your name till
with night's coming all eyes closed save mine whose every
hair pierced my scalp like a lancet. That was
not wine I drank far from your sight but my heart's
blood gushing into the cup. Wall and door wherever
I turned my eyes scored and decorated with shapes
of you. To dream of Laila Majnun prayed for
sleep. My senses came and went but neither your
face saw I nor would your fantom go from me.
Now like aloes my heart burned, now smoked as a censer.
Where was the morning gone that used on other nights
to breathe till the horizon paled? Sa'di!
Has then the chain of the Pleiades broken
tonight that every night is hung on the sky's neck?

(Sa'di)

1949

HOW DUKE VALENTINE CONTRIVED

(the murder of Vitellozzo Vitelli, Oliverotto da Fermo, Mr. Pagolo and the Duke of Gravina Orsini) according to Machiavelli:

Duke Valentine had been in Lombardy with the King
clearing up the slanders the Florentines had put about
concerning the rising at Arezzo and in Val di Chiana,
and lay in Imola scheming
      how to keep his men occupied,
      how to turn John Bentivoglia
      out of Bologna, a
      city he coveted
      to make his capital there.
      The Vitelli heard of it
and the Orsini and the rest of the gang
and it was more than they would put up with
      for they supposed
it would be their turn next,
one by one.
So they held a diet and asked the Cardinal,
Pagolo,
Gravina Orsini, Vitellozzo Vitelli, Oliverotto da Fermo,
John Paul Baglioni tyrant of Perugia,
and Mister Anthony of Venafro
representing Pandolfo Petruccio boss of Siena,
and discussed the Duke's intentions,
estimated his strength,
and said it was time to put a stop to it.
Resolved:
      not to let Bentivoglia down
      and to get the Florentines
      on their side.
      So they sent fellows
to hearten the one and persuade the other.

As soon as the news got about the malcontents took heart
throughout the Duke's territory. Some from Urbino
went out against a fortress held by the Duke's troops
who were busy hauling timber to mend their stockade
and certain beams were lying on the drawbridge
      so they couldn't raise it
      so the conspirators
hopped up onto the bridge and thence into the fortress:
upon which the whole province rebelled
and sent for their old duke,
trusting the lords of the diet to see them through,
and sent them word; and *they* thought
they oughtn't to let a chance like that slip,
      collected an army
      and marched at once
      to reduce the strongholds.

Meanwhile they sent to Florence a second time,
"the game was won already and such a chance
not likely to happen again," but the Florentines
loathed
both the Vitelli and Orsini for various reasons
and sent Niccolo Machiavelli to the Duke instead
        to offer help.
He found him in Imola, scared at the turn of events,
        just what he hadn't expected
        happening all of a sudden,
        his soldiers disaffected,
        disarmed, so to speak,
and a war on his hands. But he cheered up
and thought he might stave things off
with a few men and a lot of negotiations
until he could raise a reliable army.

        He borrowed men from the King
        and hired a few himself
        men at arms or
anybody who knew how to manage a horse.
        He even paid them.

        All the same
his enemies came to Fossombrone
where some of his men were gathered and scattered them,
so he had to negotiate for all he was worth
        (and he was a first rate humbug).
It seems "they were taking by force
        what they might have as a gift
for the title was all that he wanted,
        let them do the ruling."
Whereupon they suspended hostilities
        and sent Mr. Pagolo
to draw up an armistice: but the Duke
        kept on recruiting
        men and remounts,
sending them into Romagna to be less conspicuous.

When five hundred French lancers arrived
        he was strong enough to fight
but thought it safer and more sensible, on the whole,
        to cozen his enemies,
and worked it so that they signed a treaty
getting back their former powers
with four thousand ducats indemnity,
and he promised to let Bentivoglia alone
and marry into the family: and they,
to hand over Urbino and other occupied places,
        not to make war without his consent,
        not to take jobs in other armies.

Duke Guidobaldo had to clear out of Urbino
and go back to Venice, but first
he had all the forts pulled down
for as he judged
the people were on his side and how was another to rule them
without forts? Duke Valentine
sent the rest of his men into Romagna
and went to Cesena about the end of November
where he spent several days discussing what was next to be done
with envoys from the Vitelli and Orsini
who were with their armies in Urbino,
but nothing came of it till they sent Oliverotto
and "they would deal with Tuscany if he liked,
or if that wouldn't do, should they go take Sinigaglia?"
He replied he was friends with the Florentines
      but Sinigaglia
      would suit him nicely.

      A few days later
they sent to him that the town had surrendered
      but the citadel
would not surrender unless to the Duke in person,
      would he please come?
      It seemed a good opportunity
      and there could be no offence
      in going by invitation,
      so to put them off their guard
he sent away the French troops,
back in Lombardy except a hundred lancers
under the Right Reverend Ciandeles, his brother-in-law,
and left Cesena about the middle of December
for Fano where, as craftily as he knew how,
he set about persuading the Vitelli and Orsini
to wait for him in Sinigaglia, pointing out
unneighbourliness did not make for a durable peace,
whereas he was a man who could and would appreciate
his allies' arms and advice. Vitellozzo
was uneasy, he had learned from his brother's death
not to trust a prince he had once offended,
      but Orsini argued
      and the Duke sent presents
      and rotten promises
      till he consented.
The night before (that was December the thirtieth
fifteen hundred and two)—the night before
he was leaving Fano the Duke explained his plan
to eight men he thought he could trust,
      amongst them the Reverend Michael
      and d'Euna, the Right Reverend,
afterwards Cardinal: and charged them,
      when Vitellozzo, Pagolo Orsino,
      the Duke of Gravina and Oliverotto

should come out to meet him,
a couple to each of them,
these two to this one,
those two to that one,
should ride beside them
and make conversation
right into Sinigaglia and not lose sight of them
until they should come to his lodging and be taken.
He ordered all the troops,
more than two thousand horse,
ten thousand foot,
to be ready at daybreak on the Metaurus' banks,
a river five miles from Fano,
and on the last of December
joined them there and sent five hundred horse ahead,
then all the infantry, and after them
he himself with the rest of the men-at-arms.

Fano and Sinigaglia are towns of the Marches
fifteen miles apart on the Adriatic.
Going to Sinigaglia you have the mountains on your right,
very close to the sea in some places,
nowhere two miles away.
Sinigaglia city
stands about a bow-shot from the foot of the mountains
less than a mile from the shore. A little stream runs by it
wetting the wall towards Fano. When the road
is nearing Sinigaglia it skirts the mountains,
turns left, follows the stream,
and crosses by a bridge nearly opposite the gate
which is at right angles to the wall. Between it and the bridge
there is a suburb with a square, and a bend of the stream
bounds it on two sides.

Since the Vitelli and Orsini
had made up their minds
to wait for the Duke
and do the handsome thing
they had sent their soldiers out of Sinigaglia
to a castle six miles away to make room for the Duke's troops.
There were none left in the town but Liverotto's lot,
a thousand infantry and a hundred and fifty horse,
who were billetted in the suburb. This was how things stood
while Duke Valentine was on his way to Sinigaglia.

When the advance guard came to the bridge
they did not cross
but formed up on either side of the road in two files
and the infantry went between and halted inside the town.
Vitellozzo, Pagolo, and the Duke of Gravina
took mules and went to meet the Duke
with a small mounted escort; and Vitellozzo,

unarmed, in a tunic with green facings,
as glum as though he knew what was going to happen,
was
(considering his courage and the luck he had had in the past)
      rather admirable. They say when he quit his people
to come and meet the Duke at Sinigaglia
he took a sort of last farewell,
bid the captains look after his family,
and admonished his nephews not to rely on the clan's luck
but remember their father's and uncle's valour.

These three came to the Duke and greeted him politely.
He received them smiling; and immediately
those whose task it was were about them.
But Liverotto
was waiting in Sinigaglia with his men
on the square outside his billets by the river,
drilling them to keep them out of mischief.
The Duke noticed, and tipped a wink to the Rev. Michael
who was responsible for Liverotto. Michael rode ahead
and "it was imprudent to keep his men out of their billets
since the Duke's troopers were sure to occupy them
if found empty. Let him dismiss the parade
and come with him to the Duke."
When the Duke saw him he called out
and Liverotto saluted and joined the others.

They rode into Sinigaglia
      dismounted at the Duke's lodgings
and went with him into an inner room,
      and there they were taken;
and the Duke got straight back on horseback and ordered his scallawags
to pillage Liverotto's men and the Orsini's.
Liverotto's were handy and were pillaged.
      The Orsini's and Vitelli's
      some distance away,
      having had wind of the matter,
      had time to prepare.
      They got away
      in close order
with the Vitelli's traditional courage and discipline
in spite of hostile inhabitants and armed enemies.
      The Duke's soldiers
were not satisfied with plundering Liverotto's men
and began to sack Sinigaglia, and if he hadn't
checked their insolence by hanging a lot of them
they would have finished the job.

Night fell, the rioting abated,
and the Duke thought it opportune
to put an end to Vitellozzo and Liverotto,
and had them led out to a suitable place and strangled.

Neither said anything worthy of the occasion,
for Vitellozzo begged them to ask of the Pope
a plenary indulgence for his sins,
while Liverotto was blubbering
and putting all the blame of their treason on Vitellozzo.

Pagolo and the Duke of Gravina Orsini
were left alive until the Pope sent word
he had taken Cardinal Orsino, Archbishop of Florence,
together with Mr. James da Santa Croce:
upon which, on the eighteenth of January, at Castel della Pieve,
they were strangled in the same manner.

1933

NOTES

Notes are a confession of failure, not a palliation of it, still less a reproach to the reader, but may allay some small irritations.

VILLON III: The image of two drops of quicksilver running together is from the late E. Nesbit's "Story of the Amulet." To her I am also indebted for much of the pleasantest reading of my childhood.

ATTIS: Parodies of Lucretius and Cino da Pistoia can do no damage and intend no disrespect.

AUS DEM ZWEITEN REICH III: The great man need not be identified but will, I believe, be recognized by those who knew him.

THE WELL OF LYCOPOLIS: Gibbon mentions its effect in a footnote. The long quotations from Villon and Dante will of course be recognized. Americans may care to be informed that as a native of Paphos Venus is presumably entitled to a British passport. Her quotation from Sophie Tucker will not escape the attention of those who remember the first world war, and need not engage that of those who don't. The remarks of the brass head occur in the no longer sufficiently well-known story of Friar Bacon and Friar Bungay, of which I think Messrs Laurel and Hardy could make use. Some may remember that the only one of the rivers of Paradise to which we have access on earth, namely Zamzam, is reported to be brackish.

CHOMEI AT TOYAMA: Kamo-no-Chomei flourished somewhat over a hundred years before Dante. He belonged to the minor nobility of Japan and held various offices in the civil service. He applied for a fat job in a Shinto temple, was turned down, and next day announced his conversion to Buddhism. He wrote critical essays, tales and poems; collected an anthology of poems composed at the moment of conversion by Buddhist proselytes (one suspects irony); and was for a while secretary to the editors of the Imperial Anthology.

He retired from public life to a kind of mixture of hermitage and country cottage at Toyama on Mount Hino and there, when he was getting old, he wrote the Ho-Jo-Ki in prose, of which my poem is in the main a condensation. The careful proportion and balance he keeps, the recurrent motif of the house and some other indications suggest to me that he intended a poem more or less elegiac but had not the time nor possibly energy at his then age to invent what would have been for Japan, an entirely new form, nor to condense his material sufficiently. I have taken advantage of Professor Muccioli's Italian version, together with his learned notes, to try to complete Chomei's work for him. I cannot take his Buddhism solemnly considering the manner of his conversion, the nature of his anthology, and his whole urbane, sceptical and ironical temper. If this annoys anybody I cannot help it.

The earth quaked in the second year of Genryaku, 1185.

ODE 7: The quotation might not be readily identified without a hint. It is from Livy.

ODE 18: The war and the Forestry Commission have outdated this complaint. 'Cowpit' means overturned.

ODE 20: A presumably exact version of Jengiz Khan's correspondence with Chang Chun exists in Bretschneider's "Mediaeval Researches from Eastern Asiatic Sources." Others more competent than I may prefer to investigate it in the Si-Yu-Ki of Li Chi Chang, one of Chang Chun's disciples who made the journey with him and recorded the correspondence. Pauthier rendered that work, according to Bretschneider, very imperfectly into French.

ODE 24: The case was tried in 1917 or 1919, I forget.

ODE 32: In Samangan Rustam begot Sohrab.

ODE 33: The cool breeze of a pure, uncomprehending rendering of Handel's best known aria.

ODE 34: Perhaps it is superfluous to mention Darwin's "Formation of Vegetable Mould."

ODE 36: A friend's misunderstanding obliges me to declare that the implausible optics of this poem are not intended as an argument for the existence of God, but only suggest that the result of a successful work of art is more than the sum of its meanings and differs from them in kind.

OVERDRAFTS: It would be gratuitous to assume that a mistranslation is unintentional.

I have left these notes as they stood fifteen years ago, except for renumbering the odes where necessary.

BASIL BUNTING